PRIMARY SOURCES OF THE THIRTEEN COLONIES AND THE LOST COLONY ™

A Primary Source History of the Colony of
PENNSYLVANIA

G. S. PRENTZAS

rosen central
Primary Source ™

The Rosen Publishing Group, Inc., New York

For Nicole—

Published in 2006 by The Rosen Publishing Group, Inc.
29 East 21st Street, New York, NY 10010

Library of Congress Cataloging-in-Publication Data

Prentzas, G. S.
A primary source history of the colony of Pennsylvania/G. S. Prentzas.—1st ed.
    p. cm.—(Primary sources of the thirteen colonies and the Lost Colony)
Includes bibliographical references and index.
ISBN 1-4042-0433-4 (lib. bdg.)
ISBN 1-4042-0673-6 (pbk. bdg.)
1. Pennsylvania—History—Colonial period, ca. 1600-1775—Juvenile literature.
2. Pennsylvania—History—1775-1865—Juvenile literature.
I. Title. II. Series.
F152.P93 2006
974.8'02–dc22
                                                                                    2004028634

Manufactured in the United States of America

On the front cover: Quaker minister and artist Edward Hicks (1780–1849) painted *Penn's Treaty* around 1830. Hicks, who was born in Attleborough (now Langhorne), Pennsylvania, based his work on the acclaimed artist Benjamin West's *Penn's Treaty with the Indians* (1771–1772). Hicks used Penn's encounter, which established friendship and peace with the Lenni Lenapes in 1682, as religious inspiration because many Quakers believed that Penn's meeting fulfilled the biblical prophecy of a peaceable kingdom on earth.

CONTENTS

INTRODUCTION

An Overview of Pennsylvania's Beginnings

The Pennsylvania colony was founded with a special sense of purpose. In 1681, England's king, Charles II (1630–1685), granted a 450,000-acre (182,109-hectare) tract of land in North America to an Englishman named William Penn (1644–1718). Although Penn was the sole proprietor of the colony, which meant that he owned the colony outright, he did not view the colony only as a source of private wealth. A devout member of the Religious Society of Friends (commonly known as the Quakers), Penn wanted Pennsylvania to be a safe haven for people seeking religious freedom. At the time, Quakers and other Christian sects had faced considerable religious persecution in England and other European countries. Penn wanted to offer people of any religion a place where they could worship as they pleased.

Before arriving in his colony, Penn wrote a letter assuring the colonists already living in Pennsylvania (Swedish, Dutch, and English settlers) that he would respect their rights. He also wrote to the Native Americans, whose ancestors had lived in the region for centuries, that he sought peaceful relations with them. In a series of documents, the First Frame of Government (1682), the Second Frame of Government (1683), and the Charter of Privileges (1701), Penn guaranteed a wide range of civil liberties and provided for an elected legislature to give colonists a say in the laws that governed them.

Growth and Prosperity

Pennsylvania quickly became one of the most successful and prosperous of England's thirteen colonies. Because the colony provided civil liberties, a representative government, and affordable land, thousands of European settlers flooded into Penn's colony. Blessed with abundant natural resources and particularly rich farmland, Pennsylvania soon developed shipbuilding, iron, textiles, and glass industries, and began exporting agricultural goods. By 1710, its capital, Philadelphia, had become the second-largest city in the colonies, after Boston.

As more settlers poured into the colony, the Quaker influence began to decline. William Penn died in 1718, and his family began to care more about land sales than about Penn's vision of the colony's mission. As settlers outgrew the territory of Penn's original grant, they forced their way onto Native American lands. Peaceful relations with Native Americans gave way to mutual mistrust and, eventually, violence. When Great Britain gained control of the western frontier following the French and Indian War (1754-1763), all of Pennsylvania's Native Americans were forced out of the colony. By the time of the American Revolution (1775-1783), Pennsylvania's population had expanded to 300,000. Only about 20,000 European colonists had lived in the colony in 1700.

The Birth of the Nation

During the 1770s, Pennsylvania played a leading role in the colonies' fight for independence. The First Continental Congress met in Philadelphia in 1774 to discuss the colonies' troubles with the British government. Two years later, the city hosted the Second Continental Congress, which debated whether the colonies should separate from England. On July 4, 1776, delegates to the congress signed the Declaration of Independence, which explained why the colonies wanted independence.

The American Revolution triggered the creation of a new government for Pennsylvania, bringing about the end of the Penn family's proprietorship of the colony. During the Revolutionary War, several major battles were fought in Pennsylvania. The British occupied Philadelphia in 1777, after winning the Battle of Brandywine Creek, forcing the Continental Congress to flee the city. The Continental army spent a harsh winter in nearby Valley Forge, Pennsylvania.

A few years after the American victory in the Revolutionary War, the need for a stronger national government became clear to many Americans. In 1787, delegates from each state met in Philadelphia to make improvements to the Articles of Confederation, the framework of laws that governed the new nation. Instead, the delegates created a stronger central government by drafting the United States Constitution and sending it to the states for ratification. When it ratified the Constitution on December 12, 1787, Pennsylvania became the nation's second state.

CHAPTER 1

The Early Settlement of Pennsylvania

The first people to inhabit North America and South America migrated from Asia many years ago. Scientists do not agree about exactly when these original settlers arrived, but most estimate that humans first set foot in the Americas between 50,000 and 15,000 BC. They believe that these ancestors of today's Native Americans, or American Indians, walked between what is now Russia and Alaska at a time when the levels of the Bering Sea were low enough to expose Beringia, or the Bering Strait. These people spread throughout the Americas, arriving in present-day Pennsylvania at least 12,000 years ago. Scientists have found stone artifacts believed to be from 12,000 to 14,000 years old at a site near Pittsburgh known as the Meadowcraft Rockshelter.

By the early seventeenth century, when European explorers first reached what is now Pennsylvania, an estimated 15,000 Native Americans lived there. The largest and most powerful nation was the Lenni Lenape (pronounced leh-NEE leh-NAH-pee; "Lenni Lenape" means "original people"), who lived in villages along riverbanks from today's states of Delaware to New York. (English colonists later called the Lenni Lenapes the Delawares, after the major river along which many lived.) Anywhere from a few dozen to several hundred people lived in Lenape villages, which were notable for their longhouses, multifamily residences made of wood and animal hides. The Lenapes farmed vegetables—particularly corn, squash,

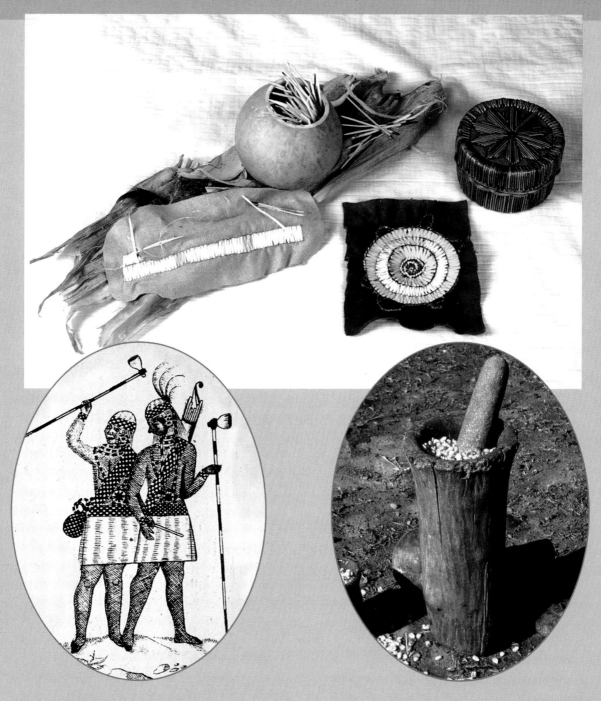

These Lenape artifacts (*top*) include a pot, clothing, a bag, and a basket that holds porcupine quills used for decoration. Peter Martensson Lindestrom, an engineer from Sweden, included this drawing (*bottom left*) of a Lenape couple, who are wearing wampum belts, when he made a map of the Delaware River in the mid-1650s. Besides collecting firewood, sewing clothing, and making pottery, Lenape women prepared most of the meals. The mortar and pestle pictured here (*bottom right*) was used by Lenape women to grind corn into cornmeal.

and beans—in fields outside their villages. They fished in rivers and streams. In the lush woods surrounding their villages, Lenape men hunted deer and other game, while women and children gathered nuts, fruits, and edible plants.

Another Indian people, the Susquehannocks, lived along the Susquehanna River (which was named after them) in central Pennsylvania. Also known as the Conestoga, they, too, lived in villages and farmed, hunted, and fished. A small nation, known as the Erie, lived near the shores of Lake Erie in northwestern Pennsylvania. By the late seventeenth century, the Susquehannocks and Eries would leave Pennsylvania after being devastated by disease and defeated by New York's powerful Iroquois Indians. Two other peoples, the Shawnee and the Monongahela, lived in western Pennsylvania. Little is known about the Monongahelas, who disappeared before Europeans arrived. Most Shawnees would move west as the European settlements grew.

Early European Exploration

The first contact between Pennsylvania Indians and Europeans is believed to have occurred in 1608. Two of the major European military and economic powers of the period, England and France, had begun establishing colonies in eastern North America in the early 1600s. The British founded their first permanent American settlement at Jamestown, Virginia, in 1607. One year later, the French established Quebec, in present-day Canada, as the capital of New France. (The French colonies of New France [1534–1763] generally included the settlements along the shores of the St. Lawrence River, Newfoundland, Nova Scotia, the Great Lakes region, and parts of the Mississippi Valley.) In 1615, New France's governor Samuel de Champlain sent Étienne Brûlé to explore the

Dutch explorer Cornelius Hendricksen drew this map of the Delaware and Hudson rivers around 1614. Hendricksen was one of the first explorers to survey this area of New Netherland. His map shows Delaware Bay at the bottom left (also seen in the detail), the Hudson River in the upper right, and the various Native American settlements he encountered in the region.

Susquehanna River. Brûlé and his Indian guides paddled their canoe from the river's source near present-day Cooperstown in central New York into what is now Pennsylvania. They may have trekked as far south as Maryland, where the Susquehanna drains into the Chesapeake Bay.

The Swedes and Dutch in Pennsylvania

France and England were not the only European countries interested in North America. In March 1638, the *Griffin* and the *Key of Kalmar*, two Swedish ships under the command of Peter Minuit (1580–1638), arrived at Delaware Bay. The Swedes established their first settlement in present-day Wilmington, Delaware. They named it Fort Christina, after Sweden's young queen, Christina (1632–1654), and started building their colony, New Sweden.

In February 1643, a new governor, Johan Printz (1592–1663), arrived from Sweden. An intimidating man, he firmly ruled New Sweden under Swedish law for ten years. Printz quickly moved the capital about 15 miles (24 kilometers) up the Delaware River to a location on Tinicum Island (just south of present-day Philadelphia) that could be better defended against colonists from other European countries. Printz named the new settlement New Gothenburg in honor of Gothenburg, Sweden. New Gothenburg was the first permanent European settlement in what is today called the Commonwealth of Pennsylvania.

Printz oversaw the construction of a fort, his residence (Printzhof), and other buildings, and he established friendly trade relations with the Lenni Lenapes. However, most of New Gothenburg's buildings burned down in November 1645, and the colonists suffered through a harsh winter. But they persevered, creating farms and small villages along the shores of the Delaware

Johan Björnsson Printz was governor of New Sweden from 1643 to 1653. As governor, Printz was responsible for carrying out the twenty-eight articles in the new charter, called the Instructions. These included directions on how the Native Americans should be treated ("with all humanity"), how the land should be cultivated, particularly for tobacco, how the cattle should be raised, and how young people should be educated.

River in present-day Delaware, New Jersey, and Pennsylvania. In what is now the city of Philadelphia, the colonists built Old Swede's Church (1643) and a gristmill. According to Albert Myers's *Narratives of Early Pennsylvania*, in 1647, Printz wrote in a report that was sent back to Sweden, "the country is well suited for all sorts of cultivation; also for whale fishing . . . if some one was here who understood the business." Despite Printz's glowing remarks about New Sweden, the colony struggled. It received little support from Sweden, and only about 600 European colonists settled the entire colony.

In 1653, Printz returned to Sweden, and a new governor, Johan Rising (1617–1672), arrived the following year. Rising soon decided to seize Fort Casimir in present-day New Castle, Delaware, to expel the Dutch who had built the fort to start a colony in the region. The Dutch had long been interested in establishing a colony in Pennsylvania. English navigator Henry Hudson (about 1565–1611) had explored Delaware Bay for the Dutch in 1609, and six years later Dutch explorer Cornelius Hendricksen sailed up the Delaware River to the future site of Philadelphia. During the 1620s, the Dutch established their New Netherland colony, which would stretch from Connecticut to Delaware. Some of their territorial claims overlapped the land that the Swedes had purchased from the Lenapes.

In 1655, the Dutch responded to the capture of Fort Casimir by sending a fleet of ships to Delaware Bay. Carrying more than 300 soldiers under the command of New Netherland's fiery governor, Peter Stuyvesant (about 1610–1672), the seven warships arrived at Fort Christina in September after reclaiming Fort Casimir. The Swedes surrendered to Stuyvesant two weeks later on September 25, 1655, and Rising handed over control of New Sweden to the Dutch.

Although New Sweden's territory became part of New Netherland, the Dutch allowed the Swedish colonists to keep their farms and homes. Dutch rule, which lasted from 1655 to 1664, had little effect on the colonists' daily life. Pennsylvania continued to grow slowly, with only a few hundred additional settlers making their home in the colony by the end of the Dutch period.

The British Seize Control

By the 1660s, England controlled much of the East Coast from Maine to the Carolinas. Its southern colonies were separated from New England by New Netherland. The British, however, maintained that one of their explorers, John Cabot (about 1450–1499), had claimed the North American lands now occupied by the Dutch in 1497. King Charles II of England sought to unite

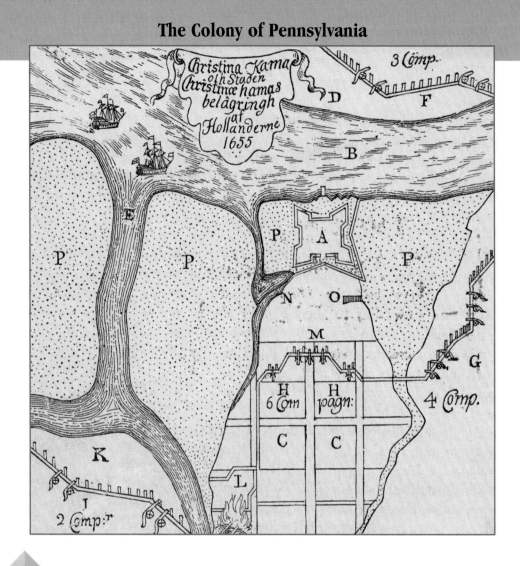

The Dutch besieged Fort Christina in September 1655. The fort (which is labeled A) and its siege (the besiegers are labeled M) are depicted in this illustration, which was printed in 1702 by Thomas Campanius Holm (about 1670–1702). Holm based the map on the manuscript and notes of his grandfather, Johan Campanius Holm (1601–1683), who settled in the colony in 1643 as its minister. When New Sweden surrendered to the Dutch in 1655, it became part of New Netherland.

the English colonies by pushing the Dutch out of North America. In 1664, he gave the territory of New Netherland to his brother, James, Duke of York (1633–1701). James sent a flotilla of warships under the command of Richard Nicolls (1624–1672) to New

Amsterdam (now New York City), the capital of New Netherland. Heeding the pleas of the city's citizens, Governor Stuyvesant reluctantly surrendered without a fight on September 6, 1664. All of New Netherland, including Pennsylvania, now belonged to England.

During the next few years, a small number of English settlers came to Pennsylvania, but the colony continued to struggle and remained sparsely populated. The colony's fortunes would change in 1681, however, when Charles II granted the territory to Englishman William Penn.

CHAPTER 2

In the late 1640s, George Fox (1624-1691) founded a religious sect in England called the Religious Society of Friends. Fox preached that Christians did not need ministers, formal religious ceremonies, or scripture itself, because individuals could find spiritual truth through an "inner light" by which God would directly illuminate their souls. In their meetings, the Friends usually worshiped silently, although anyone—man or woman—could rise and speak to the group. They lived modestly, dressed in plain clothes, and believed that all people were equal. The Friends firmly opposed war, refusing to serve in Britain's army or navy, or to pay taxes to support England's wars.

The Founding of Pennsylvania

The Friends' religious beliefs clashed with those of the Church of England and English society. Their views on war, equality, and other topics angered the government, which passed laws limiting freedom of speech and outlawing the religious gatherings of the Friends and other nonconformist groups, such as the Puritans. The Friends, or Quakers as they became known, encountered significant persecution in England. Between 1661 and the late 1680s, when the Quaker population had grown to about 60,000, thousands of Quakers were imprisoned by English authorities for religious dissent. At least 450 died during this period as a result of various kinds of torture.

Penn's "Holy Experiment"

One of England's most prominent Quakers was William Penn (1644-1718), who traveled throughout England to explain and

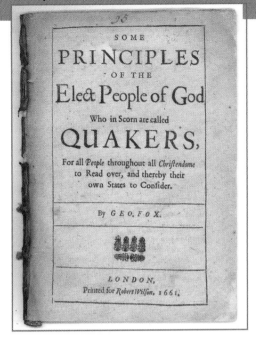

George Fox (*left*) founded the Religious Society of Friends in England when he was in his early twenties. Fox, whose parents were Puritans, became disillusioned with the established religions of his day. After having a spiritual experience, he answered the call to be a preacher. He advanced the idea of "Inward Light" or "Inner Voice," in which he believed that God's spirit was to be found within the soul of every person. At right is the title page of Fox's *Some Principles of the Elect People of God Who in Scorn are called Quakers* . . . , which was published in London in 1661.

spread his religion. The son of a rich, prominent naval hero and government official, Penn had converted to the Quaker faith in 1666, at the age of twenty-two. He strongly believed in the right of individuals to worship as they pleased. British authorities jailed Penn four times for writing religious tracts, such as *No Cross, No Crown* (1669) and *The Great Case of Liberty of Conscience* (1670), in which he defended his beliefs.

Penn realized that the Quakers would never be able to worship peacefully in England. In 1680, he asked King Charles II to repay a large debt that the king owed to Penn's father, who had died ten

THE ORIGIN OF "QUAKER"

Members of the Religious Society of Friends are often called Quakers. In *Founder's Journal* (1653), George Fox explained the origin of the term. During a trial in Derby, England, where he had been arrested because of his religious beliefs, Fox told the judge "to tremble at the Word of the Lord" (quoted in Thomas Hamm's *The Quakers in America*). The judge called him a Quaker, and soon Friends were being called Quakers.

years earlier, by granting him land in the North American colonies. On March 4, 1681, Charles signed the Charter of Pennsylvania, which granted thirty-seven-year-old William Penn a 450,000-acre (182,109 ha) tract of land west of the Delaware River, bordering on New Jersey, New York, and Maryland. Charles II named the colony Pennsylvania, combining the Penn family name with *sylvania*, the Latin word for "forest."

As Pennsylvania's proprietor, or owner, Penn had nearly unlimited power. He could select government officials, make the colony's laws, sell land, and collect taxes. He envisioned his colony as a place where people of all religions and nationalities could live together. Penn wrote that his colony would be a "holy experiment." It would show the world how a peaceful, prosperous society could be built. While he carefully made plans for the colony, Penn circulated promotional leaflets about Pennsylvania throughout England, Ireland, Wales, Scotland, Germany, and the Netherlands to attract colonists. People eager to escape religious persecution or attracted to the economic opportunities in North America bought land from Penn.

A twenty-two-year-old William Penn is pictured here wearing armor. Penn's father, Sir William Penn, was an admiral, and young Penn considered following his father's military career. Penn lived in Ireland from 1666 to 1667, and began to study law there. With his friend Lord Arran, Penn helped quell a revolt in Carrickfergus, proving his calmness and bravery under fire. Penn converted to the Quaker religion in 1666, sometime after the rebellion.

In the spring of 1681, Penn appointed his cousin William Markham as deputy governor and sent him to Pennsylvania. Along with three boatloads of settlers, Markham brought a letter from Penn addressed to the Swedes, the Dutch, and the other settlers in the territory. According to Edwin Bronner in his book entitled *William Penn's Holy Experiment*, Penn's letter assured them that he would respect their basic rights: "For you are now fixed at the mercy of no governor that comes to make his fortune great; you shall be governed by laws of your own making and live a free, and if you will, a sober and industrious life. I shall not usurp the right of any, or oppress his person."

Penn Arrives in His Colony

On October 27, 1682, William Penn arrived in New Castle, Delaware, with about 100 colonists. (Seven months earlier, the Duke of York had given the small colony of Delaware to Penn.) The next day, Penn and his followers sailed 20 miles (32 km) up

King Charles II granted William Penn the Charter of Pennsylvania on March 4, 1681, the first page of which is pictured here (*top*). By providing Penn with the colony, Charles II may have wished to expand British holdings, to repay a debt that he owed Penn's father, and to remove the Quakers to the distant lands in America. For a partial transcription of the charter, see page 55. The Great Seal of Charles II shows the king on horseback on one side of the seal (*bottom left*) and the king enthroned on the other side (*bottom right*). It was used in 1672 for a treaty. A seal such as this held the silk cord that bound the four pages of the charter together.

the river to the Dutch-named village of Oplandt. Renamed Chester by Penn, the village served as Pennsylvania's capital until 1683. From Chester, Penn traveled to the site where the colony's new capital was being built.

Penn had carefully planned the new capital before arriving in Pennsylvania. He wanted it to be beautiful and efficient. When he arrived, only a handful of houses had been built, but workers were constructing more houses and arranging the streets in an orderly grid pattern, as Penn had instructed. Penn named this town Philadelphia, which is a Greek word meaning "brotherly love."

A Representative Government

Before leaving England, Penn had drafted the First Frame of Government, a constitution that spelled out how Pennsylvania would be governed. As proprietor, Penn would serve as governor, and the colony would have a two-part legislature: an upper chamber called the Council and a lower chamber called the Assembly. The Council would have the power to propose laws for the colony, while the Assembly would vote on laws proposed by either the Council or the governor.

Pennsylvania's freemen, or male citizens, would elect members of the Council and the Assembly. This meant that less than half of Pennsylvania's adult population would vote because women, indentured servants, and slaves were not given the privilege to vote. An election was held, and Pennsylvania's first legislature met in Chester in December 1682.

In 1682, Penn also met with representatives of the Lenni Lenapes, Susquehannocks, and Shawnees to assure them of his friendship. He promised that the colonists would always respect the rights of the Native Americans. Lenape chief Tamanend presented Penn with a wampum belt that showed an Indian and a Quaker

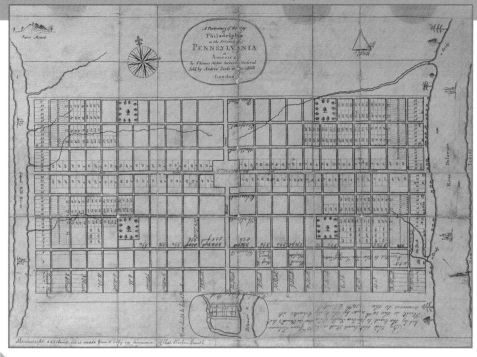

Penn hired Thomas Holme (1624–1695) as general surveyor to make this map and plan of the city of Philadelphia. The map was used to help land sales, and Penn included it in his August 1683 letter to the Free Society of Traders (a joint stock company that was formed in 1682 to invest in Pennsylvania) to help advertise the lots and to encourage people to come live in Philadelphia. Holme's gridlike map of Philadelphia was the first town plan prepared in the British colonies for a city that had not yet been built. Philadelphia was laid out on about 1,200 acres (486 ha) of land between the Schuylkill and Delaware rivers.

holding hands in friendship. (Wampum are beads of polished shells that Native Americans often strung in belts, sashes, or strands, which they used as money, ceremonial pledges, or ornaments.)

The First Frame of Government dissatisfied some colonists, so in 1683, Penn wrote a new constitution called the Second Frame of Government. It gave colonists a greater say in the government, but Penn refused requests to allow the Assembly to propose laws. The Second Frame became law in April 1683, the same year that the capital moved from Chester to Philadelphia. Penn soon returned to England to settle a dispute over the boundary between Pennsylvania and Maryland. He departed in August 1684, leaving the Council in charge. The colony's founder would not return for fifteen years.

Troubles Mount During Penn's Absence

Events in England had a tremendous impact on Pennsylvania during the final years of the seventeenth century. King James II (the former Duke of York) had succeeded his brother, Charles II, in 1685, but was overthrown three years later. England's new rulers, William and Mary, had Penn thrown in jail because they feared he remained loyal to James II. Penn temporarily lost control of his colony in 1692, but it was returned to him when he was found not guilty of plotting to overthrow William and Mary.

While Penn dealt with his problems in England, disagreements about how Pennsylvania should be governed troubled the colony. Residents of the three Delaware counties were unhappy because they had no representatives in the powerful Council. Members of the Assembly were dissatisfied that they were not able to propose laws. Personal disputes led to discord in the legislature.

The Charter of Privileges

In 1699, William Penn returned to Pennsylvania. While the Penn family took up residence in its mansion at Pennsbury Manor, Penn began to address the colony's political problems. In 1701, he wrote a third constitution, the Charter of Privileges, which pleased most colonists. It gave voters greater control over the government by giving the Assembly complete control of law-making and taxation. The charter significantly reduced the role of the governor and the Council, which had been comprised of

Penn's Charter of Privileges for the Province of Pennsylvania (1701), the first page of which is pictured here, was a revised constitution that granted the Assembly additional powers. It guaranteed the colonists' freedoms of conscience and religion, and it gave the representatives, instead of the governor, the right to make laws. The three Lower Counties, as the future state of Delaware was called at the time, got their own assembly in 1702, but the Charter of Privileges was theirs as well, as was the governor. The charter remained Pennsylvania's constitution until 1776. For a partial transcription of the charter, see page 55.

the colony's wealthiest residents. It also granted Delaware a separate legislature. The Charter of Privileges was greatly respected and would remain the law of Pennsylvania for seventy-five years. Penn then left Pennsylvania in November 1701 to defend his property against English officials who wanted all proprietorships in the North American colonies turned over to the British government.

CHAPTER 3

Although Pennsylvania's early development was slower than that of most of the other twelve colonies, it soon became one of the wealthiest and most influential colonies. Only about 500 settlers lived in Pennsylvania when Penn took ownership in 1682, but by his departure in 1701, that number had increased to 20,000. Affordable land and the rights guaranteed by the Charter of Privileges attracted many immigrants.

A Safe Haven

Pennsylvania soon became recognized as a safe haven for many immigrant groups. In the colony's early years, Quakers from England, Wales, and Ireland arrived in large numbers. From the 1710s to the 1750s, members of various German Protestant sects—notably the Amish, Mennonites, and Moravians—set up farms in the fertile regions north and west of Philadelphia. In Germany, these groups had suffered much persecution because their religious beliefs clashed with the Roman Catholic Church, so they immigrated to Pennsylvania in search of the freedom to worship as they pleased. These German settlers created their own communities, such as Germantown (Mennonites), Bethlehem (Moravians), and Lancaster (Amish). They became popularly known as the Pennsylvania Dutch. Scotch-Irish immigrants began arriving in large numbers in 1720.

These hardworking immigrants used the colonies' abundant natural resources—rich farmland, iron deposits, and dense forests—to create a prosperous agricultural, manufacturing, and

A Growing Colony

William Russell Birch engraved *The City & Port of Philadelphia, on the River Delaware from Kensington* (a section of Philadelphia) in 1800. This print shows a view of the great elm tree at the site of William Penn's treaty with the Native Americans in 1682. Philadelphia was considered the most important city in the United States in 1800, and served as the nation's capital from 1790 to 1800.

commercial economy. Through trade with Europe, the Caribbean islands, and the other twelve colonies, Pennsylvania developed a strong economy. Beaver fur trading, agricultural exports (especially flour and lumber), shipbuilding, and iron manufacturing flourished, and Philadelphia became a commercial hub.

A Prosperous City

As the colony grew, Philadelphia became a busy trading and business center. Agricultural products and other goods—being shipped to and from other colonies and overseas—filled its docks.

This is the cover of Benjamin Franklin's *Poor Richard's Almanack* of 1733. Franklin, who took the pseudonym Poor Richard Saunders for this almanac, published it annually, from 1732 to 1757, in Philadelphia. The almanac contained useful information about the weather, astronomical and astrological information, and a calendar, along with Franklin's adages that became very popular with readers. One such saying of Franklin's was "Early to bed and early to rise, makes a man healthy, wealthy, and wise."

Poor Richard, 1733.

AN

Almanack

For the Year of Christ

1733,

Being the First after LEAP YEAR:

	Years
And makes since the Creation	
By the Account of the Eastern *Greeks*	7241
By the Latin Church, when ☉ ent. ♈	6932
By the Computation of *W.W.*	5742
By the *Roman* Chronology	5682
By the *Jewish* Rabbies	5494

Wherein is contained

The Lunations, Eclipses, Judgment of the Weather, Spring Tides, Planets Motions & mutual Aspects, Sun and Moon's Rising and Setting, Length of Days, Time of High Water, Fairs, Courts, and observable Days.
Fitted to the Latitude of Forty Degrees, and a Meridian of Five Hours West from *London*, but may without sensible Error, serve all the adjacent Places, even from *Newfoundland* to *South-Carolina*.

By *RICHARD SAUNDERS*, Philom.

PHILADELPHIA:
Printed and sold by *B. FRANKLIN*, at the New Printing-Office near the Market.

The city was home to a booming shipbuilding industry, and a wide variety of craftsmen, such as blacksmiths, shoemakers, carriage-makers, bricklayers, and tailors, established their trades in the city. Financial transactions became easier when paper currency was introduced in 1723, replacing gold and silver coins. Pennsylvania's first newspaper launched in 1719, and jack-of-all-trades Benjamin Franklin (1706–1790) began his *Pennsylvania Gazette* in 1730. Two years later, his wildly popular *Poor Richard's Almanack* debuted. Arriving in Philadelphia from his native Boston in 1723, Franklin came to embody the practical, inquisitive, can-do spirit of the colony. He established a library, a firehouse, a hospital, and a school. He also served as Philadelphia's postmaster, designed an efficient wood-burning stove, invented bifocals, and experimented

THE PENNSYLVANIA DUTCH

The people known as the Pennsylvania Dutch did not emigrate from the Netherlands. Some neighbors mistakenly called these German immigrants "Pennsylvania Dutch" after mishearing the word *Deutsch*, which is the German word that means "German."

with static electricity. Franklin would later figure prominently in the thirteen colonies' move toward independence.

By 1750, approximately 120,000 colonists lived in Pennsylvania, with about 15,000 living in Philadelphia. Only one other city in the colonies—Boston, Massachusetts, with a population of 20,000—was larger. The City of Brotherly Love became known for its red brick buildings, built with bricks formed from the clay found on the shores of the Delaware River. Pennsylvania's first college, now the University of Pennsylvania, was founded in 1751 as the Philadelphia Academy.

Colonists began to build other major towns north and west of Philadelphia. The Amish founded Lancaster in 1718. Bethlehem (1740), York (1741), and Reading (1748) followed. Although colonists began encroaching on Native American lands in central and western Pennsylvania, that region was not settled until the late 1700s.

Penn's Last Days

When William Penn left his colony in 1701, he had intended to deal with his business in England and return to North America to settle for good. Once in England, however, he encountered many problems. An old debt and the high expenses associated with operating his colony put him in financial trouble. Penn also returned to an activity that he enjoyed—touring England to give speeches about his religion—but health problems soon made it impossible for him to travel. Pennsylvania's legislature and the constant complaints by colonists annoyed him so much that he offered to sell the colony back to the British government. Before the deal could be completed, however, Penn suffered a severe stroke, and the sale was never made. His second wife, Hannah, took over his business and governmental affairs, but the Assembly began making most of the colony's decisions.

William Penn died on July 30, 1718, and was buried in the Quaker cemetery in Jordans, England. He had spent only four years in the colony that he had created. After Penn's death, his descendants assumed the proprietorship of Pennsylvania. When his wife, Hannah, died in 1726, three of the Penns' sons—Thomas, John, and Richard—became the owners of Pennsylvania. They renounced their Quaker faith and focused on increasing the family fortune through land sales and taxes. The Penn family would retain possession of Pennsylvania until 1776.

Freedom Not for All

Although Pennsylvania granted many liberties, particularly religious freedom, not all Pennsylvanians fully enjoyed these rights. Women, indentured servants, slaves, non-Christians, and Native Americans had no say in the colony. As in the other colonies, women could not vote, hold public office, or own property in their own name. At the time, most people of European descent believed that men should handle business and political affairs and be in charge of their wives and daughters.

This Pennsylvania German hand-colored woodcut is called a fraktur, which is a document, such as a birth or wedding certificate or a biblical excerpt, that is written in calligraphy and illuminated with decorative motifs. Most frakturs were made by the German and Swiss-born inhabitants of Pennsylvania and Ohio. The fraktur pictured here, from around 1825, shows *Das neue Jerusalem* (The New Jerusalem) and the three paths to heaven and hell.

Thousands of immigrants worked in Pennsylvania for years as indentured servants. They agreed to work for the wealthy businessmen and farmers who paid for their transatlantic voyage to the colony. During their term of service, typically five to seven years, indentured servants had few rights, and many were poorly treated. Once they fulfilled their labor obligation, however, most were able to find opportunities in the growing colony, either taking jobs in the cities or buying cheap land on the frontier to start their own farms.

Slaveholding was not as widespread in Pennsylvania as in the other English colonies, but some Pennsylvanians, including William Penn and other Quakers, owned slaves. Many Pennsylvanians opposed slavery, however, and in 1688 some Quaker residents of Germantown submitted a petition to Quaker authorities asking that slavery be abolished in the colony. By 1700, several hundred slaves were held in bondage in Pennsylvania, and by the mid-1700s the number increased to several thousand. In the early nineteenth century, Pennsylvania would take a leading role in the antislavery movement.

Native American Relations Worsen

After Penn's death, the relatively fair treatment of Native Americans in the colony began to decline in Pennsylvania. As more and more immigrants poured into Pennsylvania, many began living on Native American lands along the western frontier. Government officials and settlers often deceived the Native Americans to take more of their land.

The Walking Purchase of 1737 illustrates one method that the colonists used to take unfair advantage of Native Americans in land deals. The Penn brothers, Thomas and John, convinced the Lenni Lenapes that a 1686 land treaty between the Lenapes and William Penn was valid, even though the document had never been signed. The Native Americans agreed to sign a new treaty, giving the Penns as much land as a man could walk in a day and a half. The Native Americans expected that about 40 miles (64 km) could be walked in that time, but the Penns hired three young, strong men to make the walk, offering a large cash prize to the one who traveled the farthest distance. Running as much as possible, one of the men covered 65 miles (105 km), between the

 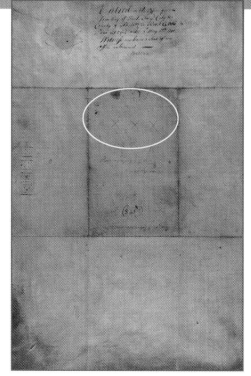

In the Walking Purchase of August 25, 1737, William Penn's sons John and Thomas and the provincial secretary, James Logan, tried to obtain the title of lands in the upper Delaware and Lehigh river valleys from the Native Americans so that they could make money in land speculation. The Native Americans agreed to give the Penns the lands that extended from a point near present-day Wrightstown, northwest into the interior "as far as a Man can goe in one day and a half." The Penns' unfair treatment of the Native Americans soon made them enemies. Note the X marks (circled) made by the Native American representatives. For a transcription of the Walking Purchase, see page 56.

present-day towns of Wrightstown and Jim Thorpe. The colony gained 750,000,000 acres (303,514,232 ha) in this deal. The Lenni Lenapes protested to no avail, and they never forgave the Penns for their dishonesty. Indian anger over broken treaty promises and land takeovers would have consequences for all Pennsylvanians.

CHAPTER 4

By the 1750s, William Penn's promise to treat Pennsylvania's Native Americans with respect had been forgotten. The Lenni Lenapes and other Native Americans were furious that treaties had been broken and that settlers had seized their lands. Many of the Lenni Lenapes, for example, had been pushed all the way into western Pennsylvania, while most Susquehannocks and Shawnees had left the region entirely. To many colonists, especially those who lived on the colony's western frontier, Native American attacks represented a daily threat to their farms and lives. They thought violence was the only solution to their problems with Native Americans.

The French and Indian War

The War Breaks Out

Since the late 1600s, England and France had collided while trying to expand their North American empires into the central United States. Between 1689 and 1748, they fought three wars over North American lands: King William's War (1689–1697), Queen Anne's War (1702–1713), and King George's War (1744–1748). These three struggles did not settle the issues between the two European powers, but a fourth conflict, the French and Indian War (1754–1763) would settle the standoff.

The French and Indian War pitted British soldiers, British colonists, and their Native American allies against French soldiers, French Canadian colonists, and their Native American allies. Because the French had been more interested in setting up trading posts than in seizing Native American land to establish

Junius Brutus Stearns (1810–1885) painted *Washington as a Captain in the French and Indian War,* oil on canvas, around 1851. Stearns depicted Washington (on horseback) leading the Virginia militia against the French in the Battle of the Monongahela River of 1755. Washington was accompanying General Edward Braddock in his march to take Fort Duquesne. Braddock was killed in the battle, and Washington's bravery under fire was later rewarded with the command of Virginia's entire militia. In November 1758, commanding several hundred troops, Washington finally captured Fort Duquesne for the British.

colonies, as the British had done, many Native Americans sided with the French. Some Native Americans, including New York's powerful Iroquois nations, sided with the British.

In 1753, the French built several forts from Lake Erie extending into what is now western Pennsylvania. In present-day Pittsburgh, they built Fort Duquesne at the spot where the Allegheny and Monongahela rivers meet to form the Ohio River. At the time, Virginia claimed this land as part of its territory, so Virginia governor Robert Dinwiddie sent George Washington, a twenty-year-old major in the colony's militia, to demand that the French withdraw from the area. When Washington returned to report that the French refused to leave, Dinwiddie sent Washington and 300 soldiers to protect British claims on the frontier. On May 28, 1754, at a site known as Great Meadows near present-day Uniontown, Pennsylvania, Washington's forces won the first battle of the French and Indian War against a small French force. Several weeks later, however, Washington surrendered when a larger French force attacked Fort Necessity, the outpost that he had built to defend his troops.

The British responded to this defeat by declaring war on France. The conflict would spill beyond the colonies, with battles fought in Europe and other locations around the world. In Europe, the conflict would be known as the Seven Years' War. Great Britain soon sent 1,400 soldiers to North America under the command of General Edward Braddock. The general made plans to capture Fort Duquesne. As Braddock's troops, along with about 250 members of the Virginia militia, approached the fort on July 9, 1755, Native Americans alerted the French of their approach. French soldiers ambushed the British brigade, killing Braddock and about half of the troops. George Washington led the retreat of the surviving soldiers and militiamen back to Virginia.

The War Strikes Pennsylvania

After this victory, known as the Battle of the Wilderness, France won several important battles in New York. The Lenni Lenapes and other Native Americans in Pennsylvania were among the tribes that joined the French side. Emboldened by Braddock's defeat, Native Americans hostile to Britain conducted many raids on Pennsylvania's western frontier, killing and abducting about 3,000 settlers and burning farmhouses and small towns. Many

JOIN, or DIE.

We hear that the General Affembly of this Province have voted

Benjamin Franklin printed this political cartoon, "Join, or Die," in the *Pennsylvania Gazette* on May 9, 1754. His woodcut, which is considered the first American political cartoon, warns the British colonies in America to join or die, meaning that the colonies must unite against the French and their Native American allies if the colonists wanted to prevail over the French threat to the colonial settlements.

settlers abandoned their farms and homes, fleeing east to Reading, Bethlehem, and other towns.

These attacks had a major impact on Pennsylvania's government. With the colony facing an all-out war, Quaker representatives resigned from the legislature. The Assembly quickly voted to provide money to build dozens of forts to protect settlers living on the frontier. Many colonists joined militias to defend the colony from Native American attacks. After three years of fighting, the Pennsylvania militia struck a major blow, defeating a large group of Lenni Lenapes on September 8, 1756, near Fort Duquesne.

The British Take the Upper Hand

Great Britain began sending more soldiers and supplies to help defeat the French and their Native American allies. In 1758, nearly 8,000 soldiers under the command of General John Forbes arrived in Philadelphia. In November, Forbes's army advanced on Fort Duquesne. Realizing that they could not repel this large force, the French blew up their stronghold and returned to Canada. Forbes had his men build a new post on the site, naming it Fort Pitt in honor of William Pitt (1708–1788), an important

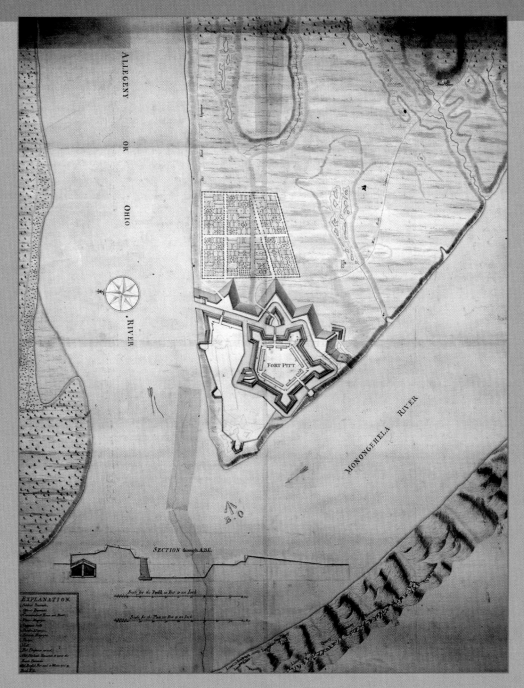

This plan of Fort Pitt, which was drawn in 1761, shows the outpost's strategic location at the fork of the Ohio, Allegheny, and Monongahela rivers. France and England both realized the importance of the site in controlling North America's fur trade and in plans for expanding settlement in the West. The star-shaped design of the fort, formerly Fort Duquesne, was based on the solidly fortified plans of King Louis XIV's chief engineer, Sébastien le Prestre de Vauban, to withstand heavy attacks.

British statesman who became the first Earl of Chatham. The town that arose outside the fort's walls was named Pittsburgh.

The British army gained more successes on the battlefield. From 1758 to 1759, it won several major battles in New York and Canada. Then in September 1759, it won the war's decisive battle in Quebec, Canada. This victory gave Britain control over much of North America. When the French signed the 1763 Treaty of Paris ending the French and Indian War, they gave the British their Canadian lands and all the territory they had claimed east of the Mississippi River, except for New Orleans and west Louisiana, which were ceded to Spain.

Skirmishes in Pennsylvania Continue

Although the British and the French had quit fighting, hostilities between Native Americans and settlers continued. Pontiac (about 1720–1769), a chief of the Ottawa Indians, organized an army that included Ottawa, Seneca, Shawnee, and Lenni Lenape fighters. In the spring of 1763, Pontiac's confederacy began attacking frontier settlements from present-day Michigan to Virginia. During Pontiac's Rebellion (1763–1765), as the conflict became known, Native Americans captured several forts in Pennsylvania, nearly overran Fort Pitt, and burned homesteads. A British victory at the Battle of Bushy Run, fought 25 miles (40 km) east of Fort Pitt in August 1763, proved to be a major turning point in the conflict.

The most tragic incident during Pontiac's Rebellion took place in Pennsylvania. In late 1763, a gang known as the Paxton Boys believed that a Native American war leader was hiding in Conestoga, a Susquehannock village near Lancaster. Conestoga was home to twenty Susquehannocks. They were the last known members of their tribe; war and disease had killed the rest of their people. In mid-December, fifty Paxton Boys arrived at Conestoga and slaughtered six unarmed Susquehannocks. All of the surviving Susquehannocks fled to Lancaster, where they hid in the local jail. On December 27, 1763, the Paxton Boys broke into the jail and killed the last fourteen Susquehannocks—mostly old men, women, and children.

In response, the Assembly voted to provide a safe haven for all friendly Native Americans in Philadelphia. Joined by several hundred other frontiersmen outraged that the government was protecting Native Americans, the Paxton Boys headed toward the capital to kill the Native Americans and, if necessary, overthrow the colonial government. Noted scientist David Rittenhouse (1732–1796) recalled them "running the muzzles of their guns through windows, swearing and halooing, attacking men without provocation . . . and pretending to scalp them." Benjamin Franklin formed a militia and headed off the Paxton Boys at Germantown. He persuaded the angry mob to put down its weapons, return home, and make its complaints through its representatives in the Assembly.

The Opening of the Western Frontier

In the aftermath of Pontiac's Rebellion, Pennsylvania's western frontier was opened up for settlement. Before the conflict, some colonists had been violating the land treaties William Penn and his successors had negotiated by settling on Native American land. After the Native Americans were defeated, those treaties were completely ignored. By the late 1760s, most of the Lenni Lenapes and other Native Americans had fled Pennsylvania. They moved west to Ohio and other locations.

CHAPTER 5

After winning the French and Indian War, Britain faced serious financial problems. It had run up a huge debt to pay for the war. Thousands of British troops remained in North America to defend the colonies against attacks by Native Americans and to control Britain's colonies more firmly. To pay its military costs, Britain's parliament passed a series of laws taxing the thirteen colonies. The colonies had no representatives in Parliament, so colonists had no input in making these laws. Colonists became angry at these new taxes, feeling that they were being treated unfairly. "Taxation without representation is tyranny" became a common rallying cry in the colonies. The British had a hard time understanding the colonists' complaints, reasoning that the colonies were merely being asked to pay for their own defense.

The Shift Toward Independence

Resisting British Taxation

The Stamp Act of 1765 was the first tax to face widespread opposition in the colonies. It required colonists to buy special stamps to attach to legal documents, publications, and other items, such as playing cards. Before the Stamp Act could go into effect, however, organized protests raged throughout the colonies. Parliament finally decided to withdraw the law to calm the colonists. Protests in Pennsylvania were rare because its leaders had tried to resolve disputes by negotiating with Parliament. Many of Pennsylvania's government officials and

This skull and crossbones image appeared on the front page of the *Pennsylvania Journal and Weekly Advertiser*, on October 31, 1765. Printed around the image are the words "This is the Place to affix the STAMP." The Stamp Act of 1765 infuriated the colonists, some of whom revolted by mobbing ships carrying stamped papers. Most colonists disregarded the Stamp Act and banned British goods in response. Britain repealed the act in March 1766.

wealthy businessmen would prove slow in joining the growing rebellion against Britain.

In 1767, Parliament passed the Townshend Acts, placing a duty on imported tea, glass, paper, and paint. Although these laws were meant as a compromise—they taxed goods traded between Britain and the colonies rather than the colonies directly—many colonists rebelled against them. A movement to boycott British goods began, which resulted in the British collecting less tax money. By the late 1760s, Parliament was forced to send soldiers to the colonies to maintain peace. The presence of British troops in their cities and towns angered the colonists, who lashed out by taunting and occasionally scuffling with the soldiers.

Boston emerged as the center of unrest in the colonies. In March 5, 1770, a mob surrounded Boston's Custom House seeking revenge for a brawl between soldiers and dockworkers a few days earlier. During the tense standoff, British soldiers fired into the crowd, killing five men. This incident came to be known as the Boston Massacre. British troops withdrew from the city, but tensions remained high.

Three years later, colonists in Boston again confronted British authorities. In 1773, Parliament passed the Tea Act, assuring the colonies that it would lower the price they paid for tea. Colonists, however, viewed this favorable law as a clever attempt to validate Parliament's ability to tax the colonies. Colonial officials in New York and Philadelphia turned back British tea ships sailing into their harbors. Three British tea ships anchored in Boston Harbor awaited the outcome of legal wrangling between the colony and Parliament. On December 16, 1773, sixty colonists disguised as Native Americans boarded the ships and tossed 342 chests of tea into Boston Harbor.

Parliament responded in the spring of 1774 by passing the Coercive Acts, also known as the Intolerable Acts. One new law closed Boston Harbor until the tea's owners were paid for their losses. The city's residents suffered greatly because they were cut off from their overseas trading partners. The other colonies helped out by sending food and supplies. Other laws allowed the British to house troops in empty buildings and gave the British king the power to appoint members of the Massachusetts Council (the colony's upper legislative body), which had previously been elected by its lower legislative body.

The First Continental Congress

As a result of the Coercive Acts, in the fall of 1774, representatives from the colonies assembled in Philadelphia for two months to discuss their disagreements with Britain. The First Continental Congress, as it was called, met at Carpenters' Hall. The delegates agreed to send a petition to ask Parliament for fairer treatment,

Amos Doolittle (1754–1832) engraved this scene of the battle at Lexington in 1775, at the start of the Revolutionary War. The depiction was based on eye-witness accounts, and shows the British troops on April 19, 1775, marching in columns in the center while colonial militiamen, standing behind a stone wall in the foreground, fire their muskets at the redcoats in the southern part of Lexington, Massachusetts. The fighting then moved on to Concord.

planned a boycott of British products, and recommended that the colonies form militias to defend themselves. Making a complete break from Great Britain was scarcely mentioned.

Parliament turned down the colonists' demands, so the Continental Congress made plans to meet again in Philadelphia in May 1775. Before this meeting could be held, however, colonials clashed with British troops at Lexington and Concord, two towns near Boston. British troops were dispatched to capture American leaders Samuel Adams and John Hancock in Lexington and to seize a gunpowder stockpile in Concord. When the British troops arrived in Lexington on the morning of April 19, 1775, they were met by a group of about seventy-five colonial militiamen, commonly known as minutemen. Shots were fired, killing eight and wounding ten of the inexperienced minutemen.

When the British arrived in Concord, they were met by hundreds of minutemen who had rushed to the town after hearing news of the Lexington battle. Outnumbered, the British retreated to Boston, with minutemen firing their muskets at the soldiers the entire way. By the time they reached safety, the British had suffered about 300 casualties. The American Revolution had begun.

The Second Continental Congress

Three weeks after the battles of Lexington and Concord, the Second Continental Congress opened at the Pennsylvania State House in Philadelphia. It sent a letter, drafted by Pennsylvania delegate John Dickinson, to King George III (1738–1820) asking that he resolve the conflict between the colonies and Parliament. This letter became known as the Olive Branch Petition because the olive branch had long been considered a symbol of peace. The congress also established the Continental army, naming George Washington as its commander in chief.

In Boston, a colonial militia clashed once again with British soldiers when the British tried to force it off of high ground on the city's outskirts. On June 17, 1775, the British won the Battle of Bunker Hill, but lost 1,054 men while the Americans suffered about 400 casualties. After this bloody encounter, King George III rejected the Olive Branch Petition, and in August issued a proclamation declaring that the colonies were in rebellion. Many colonists had misgivings about the rebellion. Some hoped that they would gain more rights, even if the rebellion failed. Wealthy

John Dickinson, Pennsylvania's delegate to the Second Continental Congress, was born in Talbot County, Maryland, and studied law in London, England. In July 1775, he drafted the Olive Branch Petition, which the Continental Congress signed and sent to King George III, giving the king one last chance to avoid a war for independence. After King George's rejection of the petition, the delegates to the congress voted for independence. Dickinson, who had promoted reconciliation with the king, refused to sign the Declaration of Independence. However, he volunteered for service in the Continental army.

merchants with strong business ties to England feared that independence would shrink their fortunes. Many of these people, known as Tories or Loyalists, hoped Britain would defeat the revolutionaries. Some colonists felt that the colonies were not prepared to rule themselves, while others feared that the British would punish the colonies if they lost the revolution.

Common Sense

Uncertainty about the wisdom of fighting the powerful British was widespread until a small pamphlet changed the views of many colonists. On January 10, 1776, Thomas Paine (1737–1809), an Englishman who had settled in Philadelphia in 1774, published *Common Sense*, a political essay that made the case for why the colonies should seek independence from Britain.

In *Common Sense*, Paine argued that colonists should not trust King George III or Parliament. He wrote, "America is not the main concern of British politics. Britain's own self-interest leads her to suppress the colonies' interest whenever it does not promote her own advantage." He urged the colonies to separate from England immediately. Paine also outlined a plan for a representative government. He endorsed the creation of a national legislature and state assemblies, both elected by all citizens. He advocated a written constitution that would guarantee the rights of everyone.

Paine showed his fellow colonists that independence was essential and could be achieved. His clear, simple writing style, forceful arguments, and message of hope proved wildly popular. People bought hundreds of thousands of copies of *Common Sense*, creating America's first best seller. Printers could barely keep up with the demand. Ministers and public speakers read it aloud for those who couldn't read.

Revolution in the Air

By the spring of 1776, the independence movement was gaining steam. On June 7, Virginia delegate Henry Lee and Massachusetts delegate John Adams introduced a resolution before the Second Continental Congress declaring, in part, that "these United States are, and of right ought to be free and independent states, that they are absolved from all allegiance to the British crown, and that all political connection between them and the state of Great Britain is, and ought to be totally dissolved." If the Second Continental Congress approved this resolution, the colonies would be taking the bold step of declaring their independence.

CHAPTER 6

Delegates at the Second Continental Congress were split on whether the colonies should declare their independence and delayed the vote until early July. In case it voted for independence, the congress selected a committee of five men—John Adams, Benjamin Franklin, Thomas Jefferson, Robert Livingston, and Roger Sherman—to produce a declaration of independence to explain the colonies' motives for separating from Great Britain. These five chose Jefferson to write the document.

The Declaration of Independence

In his Philadelphia apartment, located at the corner of Market and Seventh streets, Jefferson wrote perhaps the most famous document in American history, the Declaration of Independence. After the other committee members suggested a few changes, Jefferson presented it to the entire congress.

The Revolution and Statehood

On July 1, 1776, the Second Continental Congress met again to debate separation from Britain. At the end of the day, nine colonies voted in favor of independence. The Pennsylvania and South Carolina delegations voted against the independence resolution, while New York and Delaware chose not to vote. The delegates agreed that the vote needed to be unanimous, so they met the following day. On July 2, the four delegations that had not voted for independence decided to follow the majority. With this unanimous vote, the congress proclaimed the creation of a new nation: the United States of America. After making a few additional changes to the text, the congress adopted the Declaration of Independence on July 4, 1776. Copies of the Declaration of Independence were distributed throughout the thirteen colonies. In Philadelphia, the Declaration of Independence was read to a crowd outside the State House, and the State House's bell was rung.

Each state organized a new government. Pennsylvania quickly adopted a new state constitution, which ended the proprietorship of the Penn family by establishing an independent commonwealth. The state constitution created a one-house legislature, the Assembly, and gave voting rights to all male taxpayers over the age of twenty-one. The new state government met for the first time in Philadelphia on November 28, 1776.

The Revolutionary War

With troops already stationed in North America, Britain fought to keep its valuable colonies. The early years of the war did not go very well for the United States. The Continental army had few good officers, and it was poorly fed, trained, and supplied. The British seized New York City and its important harbor in November 1776. In September 1777, British troops occupied Philadelphia after defeating the Continental army at Brandywine, Pennsylvania. The congress fled to Lancaster and then to York. George Washington attempted to reclaim Philadelphia the following month, but his troops were turned back at the Battle of Germantown. He decided to have his troops spend the winter at Valley Forge, Pennsylvania, 25 miles (40 km) west of Philadelphia. The soldiers survived a rough winter despite having inadequate clothing and shelter and not enough food. Local farmers kept the army supplied as best they could.

The Continental Congress sent Benjamin Franklin to Europe to seek help in the nation's war efforts, and his diplomatic efforts succeeded. He convinced France to join the war on the American

George Washington, as commander in chief of the Continental army, wrote these proceedings of the war council on June 17, 1778, while he and his troops wintered at Valley Forge, Pennsylvania. In the proceedings, Washington mentioned that it looked as though the British troops were evacuating Philadelphia and moving toward New York. On June 19, Washington and his army left Valley Forge so that they could intercept the British in New Jersey. About a week later the two armies fought at the Battle of Monmouth. For a transcription of the proceedings, see page 57.

side in February 1778, and American fortunes in the war soon changed. The British retreated from Philadelphia in June 1778, and the congress returned to the city. In October 1781, the Continental army won the decisive battle of the American Revolution at Yorktown, Virginia, when the British surrendered. Franklin helped negotiate a peace agreement, and the formal treaty of peace was signed in Paris on September 3, 1783.

A New Nation

After the Revolutionary War, Pennsylvania continued to play a vital role in the new nation's politics. In 1781, the thirteen states approved the Articles of Confederation, the nation's first national constitution. Given their experience with central authority under the British, most Americans wanted governmental power to stay

THE LIBERTY BELL

On July 8, 1776, the bell in the tower of Pennsylvania's State House (today called Independence Hall) was rung to celebrate American independence. Manufactured in England in 1751 to celebrate the fiftieth anniversary of William Penn's Charter of Privileges, it cracked shortly after it arrived in Philadelphia. The bell was recast locally using the metal from the original bell in 1753. It became known as the Liberty Bell, and as a symbol of American independence, in the nineteenth century. The bell's inscription reads: "Proclaim Liberty throughout all the land unto all the inhabitants thereof."

mostly with the states. As a result, the Articles of Confederation created a weak national government, which eventually led to problems. The congress had no power to tax, so it could not pay national debts when the states refused to give it money. The states began disagreeing with each other; for example, the practice of taxing goods imported from neighboring states was a source of friction. In Massachusetts, some rural residents took up arms against the state government, run by wealthy Bostonians, in a conflict known as Shays's Rebellion (1786–1787). These events made many Americans realize that a stronger national government was necessary to ensure their new nation would survive.

In 1787, Philadelphia hosted a convention to improve the Articles of Confederation. The delegates, however, reorganized the nation's government when they drafted the U.S. Constitution. The Constitution established a republican form of government with separate executive, legislative, and judicial branches. Pennsylvania delegate Gouverneur Morris headed the committee that wrote the final draft. The Constitution was completed by

Gouverneur Morris *(left)* (1752–1816) of Pennsylvania headed the committee to revise the Articles of Confederation. At the Constitutional Convention, Morris advocated a strong central government, a powerful executive, and he opposed concessions involving the issue of slavery. He was a talented orator and writer, and much of the final wording of the Constitution is largely credited to him. The signatures *(right)* of the leading members of the Constitutional Convention included those of the Pennsylvania delegates: George Clymer, Thomas FitzSimmons, Benjamin Franklin, Jared Ingersoll, Thomas Mifflin, Gouverneur Morris, Robert Morris, and James Wilson. The members at the Constitutional Convention accepted the final version on September 15, 1787.

September 1787, and Pennsylvania had the most signers: George Clymer, Thomas FitzSimmons, Benjamin Franklin, Jared Ingersoll, Thomas Mifflin, Gouverneur Morris, Robert Morris, and James Wilson. Congress sent the document to the states for ratification. The Constitution became the supreme law of the United States on June 21, 1788, when New Hampshire became the ninth state to ratify it. Pennsylvania had become the nation's second state when it ratified the Constitution by a vote of 42 to 23 on December 12, 1787. Rhode Island became the last of the original thirteen states when it ratified the Constitution in May 1790.

The Keystone State

The Mason-Dixon Line had established the border between Pennsylvania and Maryland in 1768, and when the state's western frontier became settled in the late 1700s, Pennsylvania's current boundaries were finalized. After becoming a state, Pennsylvania made significant contributions to the new nation. It became the first state to abolish slavery (1780), and the Civil War's (1861–1865) decisive battle was fought in Gettysburg (1863). Pennsylvania's greatest impact was in business and manufacturing. Its lumber, coal, iron, and oil industries helped the United States grow into a powerful and prosperous nation in the nineteenth and twentieth centuries.

Pennsylvania became known as the Keystone State, in part because of its central location among the original thirteen states, and because it played a key role in the founding of the United States. (A keystone is an architectural term for the wedge-shaped stone at the top of an arch that holds the other stones in place.) Today, Pennsylvania has more than 12 million residents, making it the sixth-most populous state, and it continues to help hold the nation together.

TIMELINE

50,000 – 15,000 BC — The earliest known occupation of the Pennsylvania region occurs.

1615 —— Frenchman Étienne Brûlé paddles down the Susquehanna River into Pennsylvania.

1643 —— Swedes establish the first permanent European settlement in Pennsylvania on Tinicum Island.

1655 —— Johan Rising surrenders New Sweden to the Dutch.

1664 —— Peter Stuyvesant hands over New Netherland to the British.

1681 —— Charles II grants Pennsylvania to William Penn.

1682 —— Penn issues the First Frame of Government and arrives in his colony.

1688 —— Germantown passes the first antislavery statute in North America.

1701 —— Penn charters the city of Philadelphia, signs the Charter of Privileges, and returns to England.

1718 —— William Penn dies.

1723 —— Benjamin Franklin arrives in Philadelphia.

1737 —— The Walking Purchase takes place.

1754 —— The French and Indian War unsettles the
1763   Pennsylvania colony.

1763 —— The Paxton Boys murder the last twenty
            Susquehannocks.

1774 —— The First Continental Congress meets in
            Carpenters' Hall in Philadelphia.

1775 —— The American Revolution begins. The Second
            Continental Congress convenes in Philadelphia.

1776 —— Thomas Paine's *Common Sense* is published in
            Philadelphia; the Second Continental Congress
            approves the Declaration of Independence; and the
            Penn family's proprietorship ends with the formation
            of a new government for the state of Pennsylvania.

1777 —— Congress adopts the Articles of Confederation.

1781 —— The Articles of Confederation are ratified; General
            Cornwallis surrenders to General Washington at
            Yorktown, Virginia.

1787 —— The Constitution is drafted in Philadelphia;
            Pennsylvania becomes the second state by ratifying
            it on December 12.

PRIMARY SOURCE TRANSCRIPTIONS

Page 20: Excerpt from the Charter for the Province of Pennsylvania of March 4, 1681

Transcription

Charles the Second, by the grace of God, King of England, Scotland, France, and Ireland, Defender of the Faith, etc. To everyone reading this document, greetings. The King's trusted and well-beloved subject, William Penn, Esquire, son and heir of the late Sir William Penn—because of his admirable desire to enlarge the English empire; to promote prosperity for the King and his kingdom; and to encourage the Native Americans, through modesty and kindness, to join civil society and the Christian religion—has humbly sought the King's permission to transport a large colony to a place described below in a part of America not yet cultivated and planted. He has also humbly asked Our Royal Majesty to give all the described territory, with the exception of certain powers retained by the King and certain rights guaranteed to the colony's citizens, to him and his heirs forever . . .

Page 24: Excerpt from William Penn's Charter of Privileges for the Province of Pennsylvania of 1701

Transcription

. . . KNOW YE THEREFORE, That for the further Well-being and good Government of the said Province, and Territories; and in Pursuance of the Rights and Powers before-mentioned, I the said William Penn do declare, grant and confirm, unto all the Freemen, Planters and Adventurers, and other Inhabitants of this Province and Territories, these following Liberties, Franchises and Privileges . . .

FIRST
BECAUSE no People can be truly happy, though under the greatest Enjoyment of Civil Liberties, if abridged of the Freedom of their Consciences, as to their Religious Profession and Worship . . . I do hereby grant and declare, That no Person or Persons, inhabiting in this Province or Territories, who shall confess and acknowledge One almighty God . . . and profess him or themselves obliged to live quietly under the Civil Government, shall be in any Case molested or prejudiced, in his or their Person or Estate, because of his or their conscientious Persuasion or Practice, nor be compelled to frequent or maintain any religious Worship, Place or Ministry, contrary to his or their Mind, or to do or suffer any other Act or Thing, contrary to their religious Persuasion . . .

V

THAT all Criminals shall have the same Privileges of Witnesses and Council as their Prosecutors . . .

VIII

IF any person, through Temptation or Melancholy, shall destroy himself; his Estate, real and personal, shall notwithstanding descend to his Wife and Children, or Relations, as if he had died a natural Death; and if any Person shall be destroyed or killed by Casualty or Accident, there shall be no Forfeiture to the Governor by reason thereof . . .

AND LASTLY, I the said William Penn, Proprietary and Governor of the Province of Pennsylvania, and Territories thereunto belonging, for myself, my Heirs and Assigns, have solemnly declared, granted and confirmed, and do hereby solemnly declare, grant and confirm, That neither I, my Heirs or Assigns, shall procure or do any Thing or Things whereby the Liberties in this Charter contained and expressed, nor any Part thereof, shall be infringed or broken: And if any thing shall be procured or done, by any Person or Person's, contrary to these Presents, it shall be held of no Force or Effect . . .

Page 32: Excerpt from the Walking Purchase of August 25, 1737

Transcription

We, Teesshakomen, alias Tisheekunk, and Tootamis alias Nutimus, two of the Sachem's or Chiefs of the Delaware Indians, having, almost three Years ago, at Durham, begun a treaty with our honourable Brethren John and Thomas Penn . . . At which Treaty Several Deeds were produced and Shewed to us by our said Bretheren, concerning Several Tracts of Land which our Forefathers had, more than fifty Years ago, Bargained and Sold unto our good Friend and Brother William Penn . . . All those Tract or Tracts of Land lying and being in the Province of Pennsylvania, Beginning upon a line formerly laid out from a Corner Spruce Tree by the River Delaware, about Makeerickkitton, and from thence running along the ledge or foot of the Mountains, West North West to a corner white Oak marked with the Letter P, Standing by the Indian Path that Leadeth to an Indian town called Playwickey, and from thence extending Westward to Neshameney Creek, from which said line the said Tract or Tracts thereby Granted, doth extend itself back into the Woods as far as a Man can goe in one day and a half, and bounded on the Westerly side with the Creek called Neshameny, or the most Westerly branch thereof, So far as the said Branch doth extend, and from thence by line to the utmost extent of the said one day and a half's Journey, and from thence to the aforesaid River Delaware, and from thence down the Several Courses of the said River to the first mentioned Spruce tree . . . We Do Acknowledge Ourselves and every of Us, to be fully satisfyed that the above described Tract or Tracts of Land were truly Granted and Sold by the said Mayhkeericckkishsho, Sayhoppy, and Taughhaughsey, unto the said William Penn and his heirs, And . . . that neither We, or any of us, or our Children, shall or may at any time hereafter, have Challenge, Claim, or Demand any Right, Title or Interest, or any pretentions whatsoever of, in, or to the said Tract or Tracts of Land, or any Part thereof, but of and from the same shall be excluded, and forever Debarred. And We do hereby further Agree, that the extent of the said Tract or Tracts of Land shall be forthwith Walked, Travelled, or gone over by proper Persons to be appointed for that Purpose, According to the direction of the aforesaid Deed.

In Witness whereof, We have hereunto set our hands and Seals, at Philadelphia, the Twenty-fifth day of the Month called August, in the Year, According to the English account, one thousand Seven hundred and thirty-seven.
MANAWKYHICKON, his X mark
LAPPAWINZOE, his X mark
TEESHACOMIN, his X mark
NOOTIMUS his X mark . . .

Page 49: Excerpt from Continental War Council, June 17, 1778, Proceedings at Valley Forge, Pennsylvania, George Washington, Commander in Chief

Transcription
The commander in chief informs the council, that from a variety of concurring intelligence, there is the strongest reason to believe the enemy deigns speedily to evacuate Philadelphia, having actually put all their heavy baggage, cannon and stores around their transports, which have fallen down the river, and having sent across to the Jersey Shore the principal part of their wagons, containing their light baggage and a considerable part of their force, including, according to several recent accounts, almost the whole of their cavalry; their grenadiers and light infantry . . . That from every appearance the most natural inference is, they are destined for New York, either by marching through the Jerseys towards Amboy, or down the river to some convenient place of embarkation, and thence round by water but as it is far from impossible, they may only mean to draw us out of this strong position, throw us off our guard and attack us to advantage or may intend some southern expedition, these objects ought duly to be attended to—That their force amounts to about 10,000 rank and file, fit for duty.

GLOSSARY

boycott To refuse to conduct business with a person, company, or nation.

commonwealth A state. Four states in the United States call themselves commonwealths—Kentucky, Massachusetts, Pennsylvania, and Virginia—because they wish to stress that they have a government that is based on the common consent of the people.

diplomatic Having to do with diplomats, people who handle official relations between his or her own country and other nations.

duty A tax on goods brought into or taken out of a country.

flotilla A fleet of ships, especially a group of warships.

keystone The top stone in the middle of an arch that holds the other stones together.

indentured servant A person who agrees to work for another for a period of time in exchange for transportation and other costs.

Loyalist A Tory. An American who sided with the British during the American Revolution.

minutemen Volunteer soldiers who were not part of the Continental army but who were prepared to fight at a moment's notice.

nonconformist A person who did not obey the rules of an established church, such as the Church of England

persecution Continual cruel treatment, often for unjust reasons.

proprietorship A grant of ownership of a colony to a person that gives him or her the right to establish a government and distribute land.

ratify Approve; to officially agree.

sect A faction of people breaking off from a larger religious group.

torture To cause severe pain or suffering, usually as a punishment or way of forcing someone to do something.

Tory A Loyalist. An American who supported the British during the American Revolution.

FOR MORE INFORMATION

Delaware Tribe of Indians
220 N.W. Virginia Avenue
Bartlesville, OK 74003
(918) 336-5272
Web site: http://www.delawaretribeofindians.nsn.us

Independence National Historic Park
143 South Third Street
Philadelphia, PA 19106
(215) 965-2305
Web site: http://www.nps.gov/inde

Pennsylvania State Archives
350 North Street
Harrisburg, PA 17120-0090
(717) 783-3281
Web site: http://www.phmc.state.pa.us/bah/dam/
    overview.htm?secid=31

Valley Forge National Historic Park
PO Box 953
Valley Forge, PA 19482
(610) 783-1077
Web site: http://www.nps.gov/vafo

Web Sites

Due to the changing nature of Internet links, the Rosen Publishing
Group, Inc., has developed an online list of Web sites related to the
subject of this book. This site is updated regularly. Please use this link
to access the list:

http://www.rosenlinks.com/pstc/penn

FOR FURTHER READING

Burnett, Betty. *The Continental Congress*. New York, NY: The Rosen Publishing Group, 2004.

Fish, Bruce, and Becky Durost Fish. *Thomas Paine: Political Writer*. Philadelphia, PA: Chelsea House, 2000.

Fleming, Candace. *Ben Franklin's Almanac: Being a True Account of the Good Gentleman's Life*. New York, NY: Atheneum, 2003.

Fradin, Dennis B. *The Pennsylvania Colony*. Danbury, CT: Children's Press, 1988.

Heinrichs, Ann. *Pennsylvania*. New York, NY: Children's Press, 2000.

Hillstrom, Laurie C., et al. *French and Indian War*. Detroit, IL: UXL, 2003.

Peters, Stephen. *Pennsylvania*. Tarrytown, NY: Benchmark, 2000.

Stefoff, Rebecca. *William Penn*. Philadelphia, PA: Chelsea House, 1998.

Williams, Jean K. *The Quakers*. Danbury, CT: Franklin Watts, 1998.

Wills, Charles. *A Historical Album of Pennsylvania*. Brookfield, CT: Millbrook, 1996.

BIBLIOGRAPHY

Bronner, Edwin B. *William Penn's Holy Experiment: The Founding of Pennsylvania, 1681-1701*. Philadelphia, PA: Temple University Press, 1962.

Faragher, John Mack. *The Encyclopedia of Colonial and Revolutionary America*. New York, NY: Facts on File, 1996.

Hamm, Thomas D. *The Quakers in America*. New York, NY: Columbia University Press, 2003.

Heckwelder, John G. E. *History, Manners, and Customs of the Indian Nations Who Once Inhabited Pennsylvania and the Neighboring States*. 1876. Reprint. New York, NY: Arno, 1971.

Illick, Joseph E. *Colonial Pennsylvania: A History*. New York, NY: Charles Scribner's Sons, 1976.

Kelley, Joseph, Jr. *Pennsylvania, the Colonial Years, 1681-1776*. Garden City, NY: Doubleday, 1980.

Klein, Philip Shiver, and Ari Hoogenboom. *A History of Pennsylvania*. University Park, PA: Pennsylvania State University Press, 1980.

Miller, Randall M., and William Pencak, eds. *Pennsylvania: A History of the Commonwealth*. University Park, PA: Pennsylvania State University Press, 2002.

Myers, Albert Cook, ed. *Narratives of Early Pennsylvania, West New Jersey and Delaware, 1630-1707*. New York, NY: Charles Scribner's Sons, 1912.

Purvis, Thomas L. *Colonial America to 1763*. New York, NY: Facts on File, 1999.

Vexler, Robert I., ed. *Chronology and Documentary Handbook of the State of Pennsylvania*. Dobbs Ferry, NY: Oceana, 1979.

Wallace, Paul A. W. *Pennsylvania: Seed of a Nation*. New York, NY: Harper & Row, 1962.

PRIMARY SOURCE IMAGE LIST

Page 10: Cornelius Hendricksen drew this map when he traveled to New Netherland around 1614. Housed in the National Archives, the Hague.

Page 12: An oil painting of Johan Björnsson Printz by the Swedish School in the seventeenth century. Courtesy of the Historical Society of Pennsylvania Collection, Atwater Kent Museum of Philadelphia.

Page 14: Plan of the town and Fort Christina, besieged by the Dutch in 1655. Published in Thomas Campanius Holm's *Description of the Province of New Sweden. Now Called, by the English, Pennsylvania, in America. Compiled from the Relations and Writings of Persons Worthy of Credit, and Adorned with Maps and Plates*, by J. H. Werner in Stockholm, 1702. Housed at the New York Public Library.

Page 17 (right): Title page of George Fox's *Some Principles of the Elect People of God Who in Scorn are called Quakers, for All People Throughout all Christendome to Read Over, and Thereby Their Own States to Consider*. Printed for R. Wilson, London, 1661. Housed in the Friends Historical Library of Swarthmore College.

Page 19: *William Penn*, oil on canvas, a copy of a seventeenth-century portrait, perhaps painted by Sir Peter Lely (1618–1680). Historical Society of Pennsylvania.

Page 20 (top): The Charter of Charles II to William Penn, for Pennsylvania, March 4, 1681. First page of four pages, parchment with iron gall ink. Record Group 26, Records of the Department of State, Basic Documents, Pennsylvania Historical and Museum Commission, Pennsylvania State Archives, Harrisburg, PA.

Page 20 (bottom left and right): Great Seal of Charles II. The seal is from SP108/388, a State Papers document: "Full powers to Prince Rupert and others for a treaty with France and Portugal, 21 Nov 1652." The National Archives, United Kingdom.

Page 22: *A Portraiture of the City of Philadelphia in the Province of Pennsylvania* was drawn by Captain Thomas Holme, general surveyor, in 1683. Sold by Andrew Sowle, London, 1683. From *A Letter from William Penn Proprietary and Governour of Pennsylvania in America, to the Committee of the Free Society of Traders*, London, 1683. The Historical Society of Pennsylvania, Society Collection.

Page 24: Charter of Privileges for the Province of Pennsylvania, signed on October 28, 1701, by William Penn. Housed in the American Philosophical Society in Philadelphia, Pennsylvania.

Page 26: An engraving with watercolor, entitled *The City & Port of Philadelphia, on the River Delaware from Kensington*, by William Russell Birch (1755–1834). Birch's print, engraved around 1800, appeared as the frontispiece in his *The City of Philadelphia, in the State of Pennsylvania North America as It Appeared in the Year 1800*. Birch's engravings formed the first series of views of any American city. Housed in the State Museum of Pennsylvania, Harrisburg, Pennsylvania.

Page 27: Cover of Benjamin Franklin's 1733 *Poor Richard's Almanack*. Philadelphia, Pennsylvania.

Page 30: *Das neue Jerusalem* (The New Jerusalem), Pennsylvania German fraktur woodcut with watercolor, nineteenth century. Housed in the Library of Congress.

Page 32: The Walking Purchase, August 25, 1737. Record Group 26: Records of the Department of State, Basic Documents, Indian Deeds, #35, "Deed of Nutimus, Teekshakommen, et al . . . to John Thomas and Richard Penn," August 25, 1737. Iron gall ink on parchment, 29 3/8 inches x 17 5/8 inches. Housed in the Pennsylvania State Archives, Harrisburg, Pennsylvania.

Page 36: Benjamin Franklin published "Join, or Die," a political cartoon, in the *Pennsylvania Gazette* on May 9, 1754. Housed in the Library of Congress, Washington, D.C.

Page 37: Lt. Elias Meyer drew the plan of Fort Pitt in 1761. Housed in the National Archives, United Kingdom.

Page 41: Front page with the image of the "STAMP," from the *Pennsylvania Journal and Weekly Advertiser*, October 24, 1765. Housed in the Library of Congress.

Page 43: An engraving entitled *A View of the South Part of Lexington*, by Amos Doolittle, from a series of copper plate engravings, some of which have watercolor, published in 1775. The Phelps Stokes Collection, Miriam and Ira D. Wallach Division of Art, Prints, and Photographs, the New York Public Library.

Page 45: An oil portrait of John Dickinson, painted by Charles Willson Peale around 1782 to 1783. Housed in Independence National Historical Park, Philadelphia, Pennsylvania.

Page 49: Continental Army War Council, June 17, 1778, Proceedings at Valley Forge, Pennsylvania, written by George Washington, Commander in Chief. George Washington Papers at the Library of Congress.

INDEX

About the Author

G. S. Prentzas, who graduated with honors from the University of North Carolina School of Law, is a writer and editor living in New York. He has a keen interest in constitutional history, Native American studies, and the history of religions. Mr. Prentzas has edited many books on colonial history and has written ten books for young readers, including *Thurgood Marshall: Champion of Justice*, *The Kwakiutl Indians*, *New Orleans*, and a book on traditional Native American law.

Photo Credits

Cover Giraudon/Art Resource, NY; pp. 1, 17 (left), 30, 36, 41 Library of Congress; p. 8 (top) The Lenni Lenape Historical Society/Museum of Indian Culture (http://www.lenape.org); p. 8 (bottom left) © Getty Images; p. 8 (bottom right) Lenape Lifeways Inc.; p. 10 National Archives, The Hague: 4.VEL inventory number 519B; pp. 12, 19 © Atwater Kent Museum of Philadelphia, Courtesy of Historical Society of Pennsylvania Collection/Bridgeman Art Library; p. 14 Picture Collection, The Branch Libraries, The New York Public Library, Astor, Lenox and Tilden Foundations; p. 17 (right) Friends Historical Library of Swarthmore College; pp. 20 (top), 32 Pennsylvania Historical and Museum Commission, Pennsylvania State Archives; p. 20 (bottom left and right) The National Archives of the UK (PRO): ref. SP108/388; p. 22 The Historical Society of Pennsylvania, Society Collection (Of 610/1683); p. 24 American Philosophical Society; pp. 26, 45, 51 (left) Independence National Historical Park; p. 27 Rosenbach Museum & Library, Philadelphia; p. 34 Virginia Museum of Fine Arts, Richmond, Gift of Edgar William and Bernice Chrysler Garbisch, Photo by Ron Jennings © Virginia Museum of Fine Arts; p. 37 The National Archives of the UK (PRO): ref. MR 1/518; p. 43 Print Collection, Miriam and Ira D. Wallach Division of Art, Prints and Photographs, The New York Public Library, Astor, Lenox and Tilden Foundations; p. 49 Library of Congress, Manuscript Division; p. 51 (right) National Archives and Records Administration.

Editor: Kathy Kuhtz Campbell; Photo Researcher: Rebecca Anguin-Cohen